Racing Pigeons Advanced Techniques Young Birds Training

Dacian Busecan

Racing Pigeons Advanced Techniques -Young Birds Training

Copyright © 2014 Dacian Busecan

All rights reserved.

ISBN: **1502436647**
ISBN-13: 9781502436641

DEDICATION

Dear Friend.

On this book you will discover only the special advanced techniques applied by some of the best fanciers and champions in Racing Pigeons sport, in other words the.....How to Do It ....the right way in order to increase your chances of winning the top places on each and every single race .

Dacian Busecan

Contents

The weaning process.

The Darkness System explained

How to make your birds answer when called.

How to teach your birds to trap.

How to teach your birds to eat and drink from the basket.

Basket training methods.

The winning system for Young Birds Racing.

Young birds training program.

Young birds training program during the racing season.

The weaning process

For every fancier the arrival of the days when his young birds are separated from their parents are very much expected ,as from this young pigeons he will choose through different methods his candidates for his racing team .If the pigeons are allowed to develop bad habits as youngsters this will continue in their racing career .The greatest frustration that most of the fanciers have is when a bird come back from a race and sits out on the loft ignoring all his efforts to persuade him / her to come inside the loft and be clocked in.Such behaviour is the result of bad habits that were picked up as youngster ,or of being handled inappropriate when he returned from other races or training sessions.

 The training of the young birds begins from the day they are weaned from their parents , and is the fanciers responsibility to teach them exactly what he expects from them and even more. This young birds have the behaviour of human babies and what you will teach them that is what they will do. The weaning period is to be made when the birds have reached 4 weeks old and because this book is about advanced techniques I would suggest to place them in a loft where you will apply the darkening system that means that the loft must have blinding or whatever system you choose to create darkness inside the loft .

The Darkness System

The darkness will be applied every day from 6 PM - 8 AM next day ,and it will last 1 month before the first young birds race date.Applying this system you will have a much much greater advantage over the other competitors ,your birds will mature faster and they will moult all their body feathers but keep intact their wing flights which is exactly what you want.

At this time 4 weeks old you can vaccinate them against paramyxovirus followed 2 weeks after by the vaccine against salmonella. Food and water must be all the time at their disposal day and night on the floor level until you will notice that they easy pick up the grains and eat them with confidence .

On the first two days on their new location you must make sure that every young bird is drinking water by picking them up in your hand and pushing their beak into the water soon you will see that they will start drinking by themselves , you must do that at least once a day ,in their first day in the new loft and in the second day again .Because the food and water recipient will be on the floor within a week they will find no more difficult to proper feed themselves and drink water on their own.After their feeding confidence has settled in you can divide their feeding programme in two meals per day,one in the morning and one in the evening ,it is totally up to you 9AM, and 6PM would be just fine and you should stick with this hours for their entire young bird age.The hours feeding example was given but is entirely up to you when you do it as long as you keep this hours everything will be just fine.At this stage the fancier should begin to train his birds to come in for their food at his call or whistle ,the young birds will associate this sounds with feeding time ,and i strongly suggest you use them only when you feed your birds.The fancier should always make slow moves when around the young birds bangs ,and sudden movements are to avoid at all times as this will startle the birds and this is not what is wanted.

Their confidence in their master should be so high as he would be part of the flock and almost ignore him when inside the loft doing his daily activities,but as soon as he calls them for food they should come running.It takes practice before this is achieved and there should be a well known balance between giving the birds sufficient food for them to develop properly ,and restricting their food in order to maintain discipline and commands execution .

How to make your birds answer when called

The hunger is the only means of keeping young pigeons under control and it takes a few testing trials before the correct formula will be achieved.After a few days of two meals per day the young birds will quickly respond to the fancier`s call at food time and only when this exercise has been passed by all young birds you can pass to the next stage. Before the young birds can actually fly out is beneficial to get them outside the loft to let them to have a look at the surroundings.If your young birds loft have an aviary attached to it where the young birds can go in and out is very good ,if not you will need to make some sort of a little net cage that will be placed around the exit and entry in the loft some sort of sputnik is what i mean if your loft has got one it is just fine.

The idea is that the birds need to start using their loft positioning system by accessing the surroundings.If your birds are allowed to look out from the loft at an early age they will develop their homing instinct much quicker and when they will first venture in to their first flight of their life in case of flying too far from the loft they will have no problem returning to the loft. There will always be the danger of the predators being around and so for that reason do never let your birds unattended when performing these exercise

Racing Pigeons Advanced Techniques - Young Birds Training

Trapping System

One common mistake many fanciers are doing is letting the young birds outside the loft from one side (side door) and expecting them to enter the loft through a different opening .
 If your loft is provided with a trapping system whichever that may be the net cage mentioned earlier will play its role very well now ....you will need to place the young birds in it and let them exit and enter the loft through the trap ,this exercise must be performed twice per day one in the morning, one on the evening until your birds exit and enter the loft with confidence through the trap system.Young birds can be very stubborn creatures and some of us may find really difficult to get them to enter the loft by through the correct entrance when called .
To make your job even easier and for the young birds faster to learn in the first days of letting them out i would suggest to feed them right on the entry but inside the loft of course that way the first ones that will start eating

will be seen by the others as they are close to the entry ,and so they will soon be joined by the rest.

Their taste of so called freedom will come with their first flight around the loft,these birds have been born with a natural curiosity and under no circumstances you will force them to come out the loft ,let them do it at their own pace and will.Another crucial thing i would call it is to never let your young birds out in their first month on a racing day for example Saturday when most of the races take place ...what might happen is the strongest and courageous young birds might join a flock of racing pigeons passing close to your loft and be carried away by them ...some of the young birds do come back but some are never to be seen again, so why risk it .It is important not to feed your birds as you will want to let them out for an hour and then call them in for their food time .The courageous ones will be out first and soon the others will follow, keep eye on them all the time and stay between them, at this stage they will have confidence in you and they will recognize your presence .They will execute short flights from the loft to the house and back or to the closest building around the loft .

The time spent in the air will increase day after day and after two three weeks of practicing your birds which use to fly erratically at the beginning will fly now in compact formation.All this time you must ensure that the birds follow the good lessons you taught them food twice a day and answering when called inside, from
6PM - 8AM next day blindings shut, after 8AM blindings are up and the daily program

can begin : one hour training around the loft with no food or water given before,call your pigeons in ,give them food and water let them relax inside the loft until 5 PM , when you can let them out again for another hour.After 1 month of this exercise you will get to the next stage which is removing the feeders and drinkers from the loft after they finished eating and drinking.When you will see that everybody has eaten and drink water remove the feeders and drinkers from the loft and present them only when you call them in for food after the training session.

There will be occasions however,when birds will come out the loft ,fly on the roof house but do not want to start the training, some think that this indicates lazy birds ,if your birds are healthy then it should have no reason not to start the training flight,and a little noise or a flag raised in the air should give the young bird the start.Droppings are to be taken every 2 weeks to the vet from various places from the loft to check their health .As the weeks progress they will become more and more confident in their flying capabilities,sometimes disappearing for half an hour out of your sight ,with all these the birds will not overpass 10-15 miles radius in their training unless something unexpected happens that causes them to panic.This may be an attack by a predator hawk, or simply getting mixed up with other flock of birds ,it is something that everyone of us has and will go through and when this happen sometimes some birds are missing sometimes they all return nice and sound but there is not a lot we can do about it to prevent it from happening. The Flyaway phenomena happens when young birds are joining other groups of birds while on their flight and are never to be seen again ,nobody really knows why they are doing it but something or somewhat do determine young birds to join other flocks and the main thing to blame is overcrowding in the loft.Remember that racing pigeons are descendants of Rock Doves ....this Rock Doves in nature will live and nest on the cliffs crevices ,when the colony reaches such numbers that the colony is no longer sustainable by the available food some of them will fly away in search for other territories where they will start a new colony.From the young birds point of view this is part of their life experience and if they will pass this first test successfully they will know what to do next time if they encounter the same test again.

Remember my dear friend that at this point of your young birds training the majority of losses will occur ,so do not get disappointed when this happens no matter how well you have matched the pairings or how good you trained them so far this things are happening to all of us.I do not advise you to train your birds on the rainy days although they might encounter this weather conditions when the racing season starts ,in these days they can relax in the loft and you can spend the time that you normally spent on each training day with them in the loft by taking a closer look at your birds .These checkings should be made as often as possible , because the best advice that i could give you is that it is always better to prevent something than to cure it .

Check their feathers and see if they have any broken flights

Check their breastbone which must be straight,

The skin colour along the breastbone should be pink.

Their vents should get tighter and stronger when little pressure is applied over them

Warm feet,

Clear throat

<u>White wattles</u>

Silky feathers,

when you hold a pigeon in your hands you should have the impression of slipping him through your fingers you can read a lot more about how a pigeon should feel on the Hand Bird Selection book when it will be ready ,i really do not want to talk too much about this subject here as this book subject is young birds training only .

Basket Training

Basket training is a very debated topic between pigeon fanciers and is a question of when the formal training of young birds should begin and mostly how much experience the birds should have before the first race .The point at which the birds will be ready for their first basket training is determined by the age of the birds and the experience they have gained so far. For you to be ahead of the competition you will need to pair your stock birds 1 month before the current year`s identification rings are available ..so for example if the rings are available in the 15 of Jan 2014 you will need to start mating your stock birds at around 10 of December 2013 .

Like nearly everything in racing pigeon sport it is a question of getting the right balance and it is only with experience that the fancier learn to read the signs that tells him whether his birds needs more or less training.
 Young birds have a lot of energy and in appearance is hard to over train them but there is no point of exaggerating with 2 or 3 trainings per day which is also very costly for

the fancier himself. Winning a race does not depend only by the training the young bird has at that particular time it is a combination of factors and these are: health ,training, motivation ,feeding, loft health ,and a little bit of luck maybe. The proper basketing training should start 1 month before the first race which in theory should be at the end of July , but until then there are other steps you need to do in order to increase your chances of winning the races and i will describe them below.Before you take your young birds on the first basket training session you must make your birds get accustomed with the basket itself .It is a frightening experience for a young bird to be put into a training basket together with other birds as pigeons do not congregate naturally in such close proximity to each other and to force them to stand shoulder to shoulder in a confined space will cause distress.They will start fighting with each other and will try to escape through the basket openings ...do not let them learn this lesson the hard way there is something you can do to overcome this and avoid this unnecessary stress caused to you birds.

First thing you can do is ,one week before the first basket training you will leave the basket open inside the loft day and night so the birds can explore it ..go in and out of it... and in the last two nights you will lock them inside and in the morning release them from the basket outside the loft ,take the basket back in the loft and leave it open so the birds can explore it back again after the round the loft training has finished .

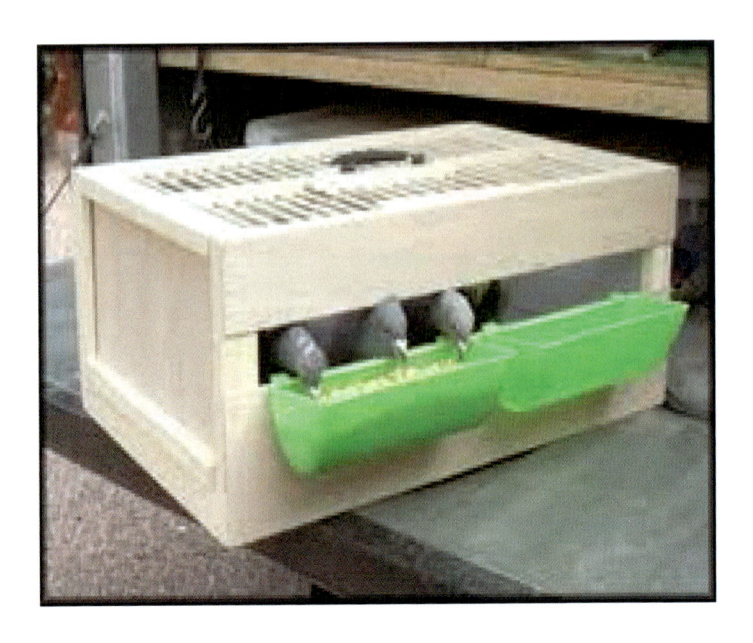

Eating and drinking from the basket

These training baskets should be equipped with drinking troughs which clip on to the outside allowing the birds to stick their heads to drink water ,food will be supplied on the races where the birds will spend more then one night in the basket and it will be served to the birds in the empty drinkers,so it is an extremely important training your birds must perform if you want them to succeed in the races to come .To teach them this you will lock young birds overnight in the basket and in the morning you will serve their food in the clipped drinkers, first the food and then the water ...the quantity of the food does not need to be the normal thing you give them when they return from training ...half will do it remember this training is to teach your birds from where they can eat and drink and not getting saturated from, especially if next day you want to take them to a road basketing training.Now that your birds have learned how to drink and feed themselves from the clipped drinkers and on the same time they are very comfortable with the basket you can start their first road basketing training.I can recommend you to start your first basketing training from 10km on a very clear blue sky morning the direction where you take them does not matter as long as they don't have to cross a 2000 m mountain ...put the basket in your trunk go to the destination, the place where you will release them from should be clear of wires ,high trees ,prey birds on the sky and especially the day you do this must not be a day race like Saturday or Sunday or whatever.

Ideally would be an open field, take the basket out from the trunk and wait for 10 minutes after that you can release them. Remember this are not the proper trainings the special trainings that will prepare them for the racing season will start 1 month before the racing season starts.

The next day the pigeons will train around the loft. The third day the distance will be 15 km in the same direction. Fourth day training around the loft. Fifth day the distance will be 20 km in the same direction. Every time you plan a basket training for your birds i recommend you feed them half quantity of food and water from the basket in that particular day. Three trainings per week up to maximum 30 km would be enough for the young birds, keep eye on their developing as this will happen fast on the darkness system. The real training starts one month before the first race as i mentioned and i would do it as it follows.

The winning system for Young Birds Racing.

If by now you have trained your birds from all directions these trainings i recommend you make them from the same direction with the release point of the first race .

Week 1

day 1 - 30 km
day 2 - 35 km
day3 - 40 km
day 4 - 45 km
day 5 - 50 km
Saturday and Sunday round the loft training.

Week 2

Start with 40 km in the first day and go up to 60 on the day5.On these two weeks it would be good to make these trainings early in the morning say 6 o clock so you can release your birds for the around the loft training at 5- 6 PM.Saturday and Sunday round the loft training.

Week 3

Now this is little bit different and i suggest you do it according to your pigeons fitness if you see your birds are fit then you can follow this:

day 1 -.......30 km at 6am .... 30 km at 4pm
day 2......35 km at 6 am ....35 km at 4pm
day 3.......40 km at 6..........40 km at 4pm
day 4........40 km at 6..........40 km at 4pm
day 5.........45km at 6...........45 km at 4pm

Saturday and Sunday – round the loft training. I think you have noticed the difference, there are two trainings per day, keep eye on the birds as you do not want to over train or fatigue them ,if you see they do not respond very well resume to one training per day to maximum 70 km in the day 5.If your birds respond well follow this on the last week before the first race.

Week 4

day1... 40 km in the morning ....40km in the afternoon
day2... 45 km in the morning ....45km in the afternoon. In the next two days you will need to do something that will put your young birds in the same situation as in the day race and what i mean by that is to make the morning training together with another fancier or even better, fanciers .It is very possible that the club where you are a member to organize this training prior to the first race and this exercise is very important as your pigeons will have to split from the flock upon their arrival home which is exactly what will happen on the day race.

day3.....6AM - 50 km combined..4PM -30km yourself.
day 4 ...6AM - 50 km combined..4PM-30km

yourself.

If your birds does not respond well with two trainings per day i suggest one morning training for the first two days for up to 70 km and the last two days one morning training combined again for up to 60 km.

day five -stop .....it is the race basketing day the birds are relaxing inside the loft all day until you basket them and send them to their first race .

Training during the racing season

After the racing season has started you will enjoy your first result .According to their arrival ,fitness and their recovery period you can start the young birds training after the first race has finished.

Monday – training around the loft on the morning at 6 AM and at 6PM on the afternoon .Do not force your birds to come out the loft if they do not have the desire to do it ,this process should happen naturally if they have recovered from the race .

If for any reason some birds do not to come out the loft it would be a good idea to go and check them individually .Stiff pectoral muscle suggest extenuation and effort over their limit,these birds will be normally the ones that came in late or in the second day of the race and will take a little bit longer to recover from the effort.The rest of the team may carry on with the normal training which will be Monday and Tuesday training around the loft on the morning and on the afternoon and for the Wednesday and Thursday you can follow the week 3 program .After the second race has ended you can start weekly training following week 3 program right from Monday again taking in consideration their recovery period from the race with relaxing on Friday.

 As i mentioned earlier in this book to win a race you must meet a combination of factors all at their peak: health,training,feeding, motivation,the loft...on this chapter you studied the training factor only please take a look at the other books i already have written, or i will publish them when you have time and combine them all together to obtain the results you expect from your birds .

It was with great pleasure that i have written all this for you my friend and i truly hope that it will help you in your racing pigeon career.

" A true fancier is the one who`s birds are always on top, whether they race under his management or somebody else`s generation after generation, a true fancier is the one who love competitions and speak highly about his competitors ...Above all ,a true fancier is the one who teach others into the sport and gladly talk about his winning ways ".

Dacian Busecan

Printed in Great Britain
by Amazon